The Inuit
Thought of It

The Inuit Thought of It

AMAZING ARCTIC INNOVATIONS

Alootook Ipellie

with David MacDonald

annick press
toronto + new york + vancouver

We acknowledge the support of the Canada Council for the Arts, the Ontario Arts Council, and the Government of Canada through the Book Publishing Industry Development Program (BPIDP) for our publishing activities.

Cataloging in Publication

Ipellie, Alootook, 1951-
          The Inuit thought of it : amazing Arctic innovations /
Alootook Ipellie with David MacDonald.

(We thought of it)
Includes bibliographical references and index.
ISBN 978-1-55451-088-7 (bound)
ISBN 978-1-55451-087-0 (pbk.)

          1. Inuit—Material culture.   2. Inuit—Intellectual life.
I. MacDonald, David, 1961- II. Title.   III. Series.

E99.I7I658 2007   303.48'30899712   C2007-902681-8

Distributed in Canada by: Published in the U.S.A. by:
Firefly Books Ltd.   Annick Press (U.S.) Ltd.
66 Leek Crescent   Distributed in the U.S.A. by:
Richmond Hill, ON   Firefly Books (U.S.) Inc.
L4B 1H1   P.O. Box 1338
                                   Ellicott Station
                                   Buffalo, NY 14205

Watch for more books in the *We Thought of It* series, coming soon.

Printed in China.

Visit us at: www.annickpress.com

For my daughter, Taina Lee, with love, and to the Ipellie family.
          —A.I.

For my parents, with love and gratitude.
          —D.M.

A sincere thank-you to expert reader Dr. David Morrison, Director of Archaeology and History, Canadian Museum of Civilization, for sharing his insight, profound knowledge, and clarity.

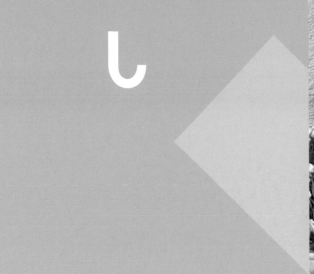

Contents

The Inuit, My People

Imagine living in a land where the temperature stays above freezing for only a couple of months each year, and where winter temperatures sometimes drop below -50°C (-58°F). What would it be like to live in a place where there is 24-hour darkness for weeks on end every winter, and 24-hour daylight for much of the summer? There is such a land, and it is like few places on earth.

Almost no trees grow here, and much of the ground is permanently frozen. Large areas of the landscape are nothing but bare rock. You could travel for days and not see a single sign that humans had ever set foot here. This land is the Arctic, and my people, the Inuit, have lived here for hundreds of years.

History of the Inuit

Many archaeologists believe that the ancient ancestors of today's Inuit may have come to North America about 20,000 years ago, crossing a land bridge that once connected Siberia and Alaska. They settled on the northwestern coast of Alaska. About 1200 years ago, the direct ancestors of the Inuit began to move east and gradually spread through the Canadian Arctic and into Greenland. In some places they would have met hunters from Viking settlements in Greenland. After these Viking settlements disappeared about 600 years ago, Inuit were the only people in the North American Arctic.

Adapting to the Land and the Climate

The first Alaskan Inuit lived on what the land had to offer. They built houses of sod and driftwood, and created a variety of hunting tools from the materials at hand. Seals, walrus, whales, and caribou provided them with food, clothing, and materials to make tools. As Inuit moved east, they brought with them traditional knowledge about making hunting tools and building sod houses. But whenever necessary, they adapted traditions to new living conditions. For example, when driftwood was not available for building a sod house, they used whalebone instead.

About 500 years ago, when the climate began to grow colder, many Inuit who lived in coastal areas of the northern Arctic began to move south. Whales were not as plentiful in the south, so Inuit adapted their lifestyle. They relied more on other sources of food, and began to move their camps more often in search of good hunting grounds. Being on the move meant that Inuit needed temporary shelters to protect them from the winter cold. They relied on the igloo, which was easy to build and could be constructed anywhere.

A Time of Change

When the first European explorers came to the Arctic in the 1500s, they did not have much effect on traditional Inuit culture. But in the 1800s, European hunters began to arrive. They came because whale products and animal furs were in demand back in Europe. Contact with Europeans, as well as with missionaries and Canadian government officials who came in the 1900s, brought many changes to how Inuit lived. As fewer people lived a traditional lifestyle, the old Inuit ways were forgotten by many. But today, Inuit are working to preserve and maintain the old traditions so that they are not lost forever.

The Inuit Spirit of Innovation

Their ability to adapt and make innovations enabled Inuit to survive in the difficult conditions of the Arctic. Of the innovations presented in this book, which are all from the period before contact with Europeans, many are truly amazing. And some of them—such as the Inuit-style parka, the kayak, and the double-bladed paddle—are now used around the world.

Enjoy your journey through the world of amazing Inuit innovations. I hope this book will make you interested in learning more about my people, our culture, and our heritage.

Timeline
Inuit and Their Ancestors in North America

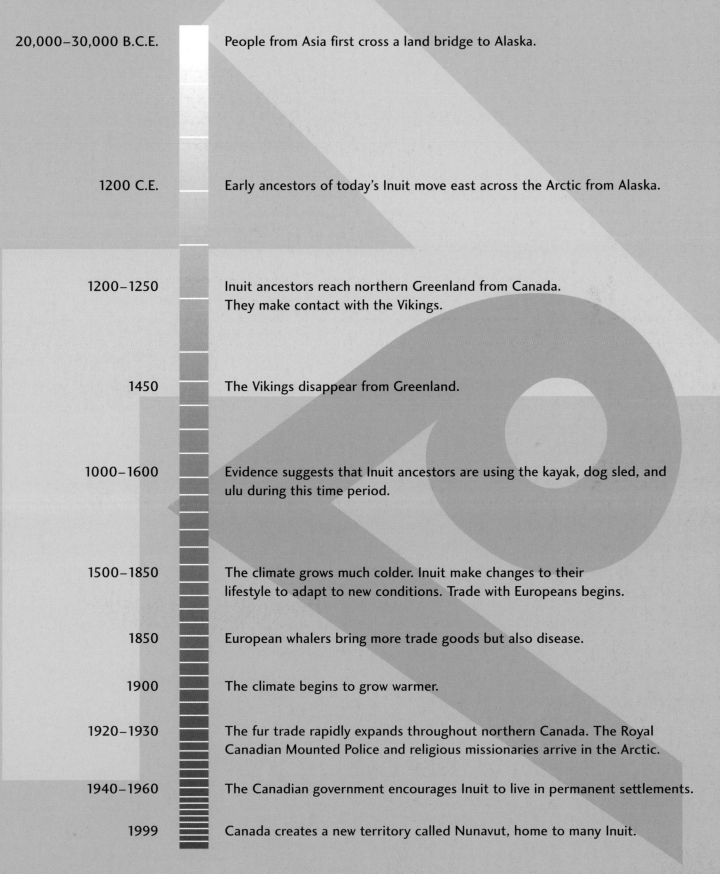

20,000–30,000 B.C.E.	People from Asia first cross a land bridge to Alaska.
1200 C.E.	Early ancestors of today's Inuit move east across the Arctic from Alaska.
1200–1250	Inuit ancestors reach northern Greenland from Canada. They make contact with the Vikings.
1450	The Vikings disappear from Greenland.
1000–1600	Evidence suggests that Inuit ancestors are using the kayak, dog sled, and ulu during this time period.
1500–1850	The climate grows much colder. Inuit make changes to their lifestyle to adapt to new conditions. Trade with Europeans begins.
1850	European whalers bring more trade goods but also disease.
1900	The climate begins to grow warmer.
1920–1930	The fur trade rapidly expands throughout northern Canada. The Royal Canadian Mounted Police and religious missionaries arrive in the Arctic.
1940–1960	The Canadian government encourages Inuit to live in permanent settlements.
1999	Canada creates a new territory called Nunavut, home to many Inuit.

Inuit in North America around 1600 C.E.

The shaded area on this map shows where Inuit were living in North America about 400 years ago.

GREENLAND

ALASKA
(USA)

CANADA

Pacific
Ocean

UNITED STATES
OF AMERICA

Atlantic
Ocean

MEXICO

This map shows all of North America today.

DOG SLEDS

In winter, when the ground was covered with snow and ice, traditional Inuit often traveled by a sled called a *qamutiik* that was pulled by a team of dogs. Sealskin rope was essential to making harnesses for the dogs and a whip to direct the dog team, and for the *qamutiik* itself.

Today, dog sled racing is a popular Arctic sport.

Sometimes Inuit helped dogs pull the sled.

Dog Boots

To pull a sled all day, the dogs' paws needed to be in good condition. Their paws were tough, but they could still get cuts from jagged ice or sharp rocks uncovered by melting snow in springtime. With injured paws, the dog team could not run as quickly. To protect their paws, Inuit often made dog boots out of seal or caribou skin.

Rope

The thick skin of the bearded seal (see photo on page 10) was best for making strong rope. First, the skin was removed by cutting it into sections. Then it was boiled and cut into long strips while still wet. The wet strips were tied between two large stones and left to dry into strong rope.

Sled

The sled runners (the long pieces that touched the ground) and the crosspieces that held the two runners together were most often made of wood. These were tied together with rope in a way that allowed each runner to move slightly up or down when traveling over uneven surfaces. Rough ground, snow, or ice could cause damage to a sled. Rope made the sled more flexible so it would last longer.

Bow-Drill

Traditional Inuit used wood and sometimes walrus tusk ivory to build the *qamutiik*. To drill holes in these materials, they invented a very useful tool called the bow-drill, which had five parts:

1. the **drill stick** (vertical piece) was made of wood or caribou antler
2. the **mouthpiece** at the top of the drill stick was made of ivory or hard wood
3. the metal **drill bit** was at the bottom of the drill stick
4. the **bow** (horizontal piece) was made of wood or antler
5. the **bowstring**, which attached the bow to the drill stick, was made of sealskin

To work the bow-drill, the user moved the bow stick back and forth with one hand.

A dog sled rests on wooden blocks.

Mud Runners

Adding mud to the runners allowed them to slide more easily over snow and ice. With the sled turned upside down, wet mud was spread over the bottom of the runners and carefully smoothed out. Then mouthfuls of water were squirted onto a piece of polar bear skin, and the wet skin was rubbed over the frozen mud. This left a layer of ice on top of the mud, so that the runners were very smooth and slippery. Mud runners made it easier for dogs to pull a heavily loaded sled.

Ivory Runners

In areas of the Arctic where walrus could be hunted, traditional Inuit sometimes made sled runners from walrus tusk ivory. Ivory is very smooth, so ivory runners didn't need the mud-and-ice coating that made wooden runners so much work. And ivory runners had two other advantages over mud runners —they didn't easily break off and they didn't melt if left in direct sunlight, as mud runners sometimes did.

A hunter prepares mud runners for his dog sled.

KAYAK

The kayak (or *qajaq*) is a long, narrow boat that is usually at least 6.5 meters (22 feet) long and 75 centimeters (30 inches) across at the widest part. A well-made traditional kayak was strong enough to carry an adult hunter and a freshly killed seal to shore. If the water was not too rough, sometimes a child would ride behind the adult, facing backward.

Like the kayak, the *umiak* also had a wooden frame.

Animal skins were often stretched and dried before use.

The Frame

The frame of a traditional kayak was made mostly from driftwood, and sometimes caribou antler and caribou bone as well. Sealskin rope and caribou sinew were used to join the pieces of the frame together. The long paddle, which had a blade at each end, was also made of wood.

The Outer Covering

The waterproof outer layer of the traditional kayak was made from sealskin. The skins were first put in hot water, then the hair was quickly scraped off while the skin was still hot. After scraping, the skins were stored in a sealskin bag along with some seal fat to keep them flexible and easy to work with.

When enough skins had been prepared, they were stretched over the frame and roughly stitched together to form an outer covering for the kayak. Excess skin was trimmed away. Tightly knotted sealskin rope held the skins in place as they dried and hardened to form a tight covering over the frame.

Next, caribou sinew was used to sew this outer covering onto the frame. After this, every seam was rinsed in seawater before one final tight stitching. It was a good idea to put some old skins inside the frame of a new kayak to prevent sand from wearing holes in the outer covering.

Inuit women stitch sealskins onto the wooden frame of a kayak.

The streamlined shape of the kayak allowed it to glide easily through the water.

Umiak

When it was time to move from one coastal camp to another, a much larger boat called an *umiak* was used to transport such things as tents, sealskin and caribou clothing, cooking equipment, and tools. An *umiak* could also carry a number of Inuit, along with their dogs, at the same time. Because women usually did the paddling, the *umiak* was sometimes called "the women's boat."

An *umiak* could carry several Inuit.

When there was wind, a sealskin sail could be used to help propel the *umiak*.

Modern Kayaks

Today, kayaks are usually made from hard plastic, although the outer covering may be fiberglass. Like traditional Inuit kayaks, modern kayaks have a streamlined shape and are made in different lengths, depending on the purpose. Longer kayaks are steadier on the sea, while shorter kayaks are easier to handle on lakes and rivers.

SHELTER

A winter home was important for surviving freezing Arctic temperatures. But in some areas, materials for building a warm home were hard to find. Traditional Inuit in these places built snow homes called igloos (or *iglu*). Strong igloos could be made only from snow that had become hard enough to walk on without breaking through. An igloo could be built almost anywhere in the snow-covered Arctic, even at a hunting camp on sea ice.

A woman carries caribou meat out of her igloo. The entrance was built below ground level to help keep cold air from getting in.

Walls and Window

An igloo was built by first carving out rectangular snow blocks about 10 centimeters (4 inches) thick. Next, these blocks were arranged in a circle to form the base of the igloo. A second layer of blocks was then stacked on top of the first. These blocks were angled inward so that, as the igloo was built upward, the blocks would form a dome. When completed, the snow dome was strong enough for an adult to climb on top without falling through. A block of lake ice was used as a window to let light inside.

Insulation and Entrance

Once the igloo's dome was built, family members would help make it windproof. On the outside, they filled in the cracks between the blocks with loose snow. For even more insulation from the cold, the outside of the whole igloo was then packed with an extra layer of more loose snow. Finally, an entrance tunnel was carved, usually just under ground level to keep cold air from getting inside. A small porch of snow blocks was then built over this entrance tunnel to provide more protection against freezing winds. An opening in the roof of the porch allowed cold air to escape before it had a chance to enter the dome of the igloo.

Community Igloo

Whenever a group of Inuit families stayed in one camp for the whole winter, they would build a *qaggiq*. This was an igloo large enough to hold all members of the camp during group gatherings.

Seal-Oil Lamp

In some places, Inuit were able to find soapstone. This soft stone was easy to carve into a bowl that could be used for a seal-oil lamp (*qulliq*). One end of a wick made from moss was dipped into the bowl of seal oil. When the other end was lit, the lamp provided light and heat inside an igloo or a skin tent.

When the igloos melted in the spring, Inuit returned to their summer camp and went back to living in tents made from caribou skin and sealskin. These shelters were used during spring, summer, and autumn.

Traditional Inuit used a bow-drill (see page 13), with the drill bit removed, or other similar inventions to produce fire. The drill stick was rotated quickly while it was pushed down upon. This created friction, which produced enough heat to start a flame.

While a lit *qulliq* could not be placed too close to a snow wall, its heat actually helped to strengthen an igloo. The heat from the *qulliq* and the body heat of the Inuit in the igloo created a thin layer of melted snow on the inside of the wall. When the Inuit extinguished the lamp and went to sleep, this layer would freeze, making the walls even stronger.

Sleeping Bag

Sleeping bags were made from caribou skin. They were sometimes large enough for two or more people, which was warmer than sleeping alone. Inside the igloo, Inuit made a snow platform and covered it with twigs and then layers of thick animal skins before placing the sleeping bag on top.

Even the beds are made from ice in this ice hotel in Kiruna, Sweden.

Building with Snow and Ice Today

Today, buildings made from snow, ice, or both are popular at winter festivals in countries such as Canada, Sweden, and Norway.

CLOTHING

In the Arctic, animals provided the only materials available for making clothes. Traditional Inuit used animal skins and fur to create warm clothing that helped them to survive in the harsh Arctic climate.

Waterproof Clothing

Inuit sometimes used a marine mammal's inside parts, such as the bladder or intestines, to make waterproof clothing. When hunting on the ocean, traditional Inuit wore a type of jacket that could be tied around the opening of the kayak. This kept the hunter's whole body dry.

Parka

The traditional winter parka, called a *qulittaq*, was essential for protecting the upper body from dangerously cold temperatures. Parkas were made from the skin of caribou hunted in the autumn, when their fur was starting to get thick for winter. Thicker fur made a warmer parka, but winter caribou fur was too heavy to wear comfortably.

This waterproof coat is made from whale intestines.

Walrus intestine was also an excellent waterproof material. To help dry the intestine, air was blown inside to inflate it, as seen here.

Baby-Carrying Parka

Inuit mothers used a special belt to carry a baby on their back. When going outdoors, mothers also wore an *amaut*, a parka with an extra-large hood. The mother's body heat kept the baby warm, and the hood's fur trim helped to keep out cold winds. This clever design allowed a mother to carry her baby while leaving her hands free to do other things.

Bird-Skin Parkas

In areas where caribou were scarce, Inuit would make parkas from the skin and feathers of water birds such as ducks or loons. The Inuit shown at left are wearing duck-skin parkas.

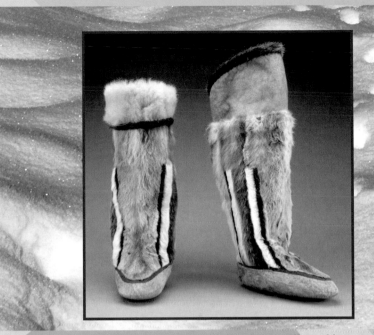

These winter boots are made from caribou skin.

To prepare sealskin for making boots, the dried skin was chewed to make it softer. Another way was to stretch the skin flat and then stomp on it with bare feet or while wearing sealskin boots.

Boots

Inuit boots, called *kamiik*, were traditionally made from pieces of sealskin sewn together with caribou sinew. Both the sealskin and the sinew were kept wet while the boots were being sewn. When they dried, the seams tightened and became waterproof.

Winter boots were made from caribou skin or the skins of seals that had the thickest fur. Light and dark furs were sewn together to make striped patterns. Girls' and women's boots traditionally had horizontal stripes from the ankle to the top of the boot. Boys' and men's boots had vertical stripes (as in the photo above).

For summer, boots were made from sealskin with the fur scraped off so they wouldn't be too warm.

Parkas Today

Modern parkas are often based on the traditional Inuit design. Many have a hood trimmed with fur, and some hoods are also lined with real or artificial fur for warmth. Like the traditional parka, modern parkas are made to fit loosely, allowing clothing to be worn underneath while still leaving room for a layer of warm insulating air.

ARCTIC FUN

Inuit children learned traditional games and pastimes from their elders. Often these forms of entertainment helped young people develop the skills and strength they would need as adults.

Sports and Games

Outdoor games were popular in summer, and in winter when the weather permitted. Both old and young, males and females, joined in the fun. Over time, some traditional Inuit games became similar to sports such as baseball and soccer. There is even an Inuit form of football, called *ajuttaq*.

Winters are long and dark in the Arctic. To pass the time, Inuit traditionally gathered together to take part in a variety of contests. Along with different kinds of wrestling, contests might include such favorites as the "toe jump" and the "finger pull." All the activities required strength and endurance.

It's not surprising that this game is known as the "two-foot high kick."

Today, Inuit gather every other year to compete in the Arctic Winter Games. This contestant is competing in the "toe jump."

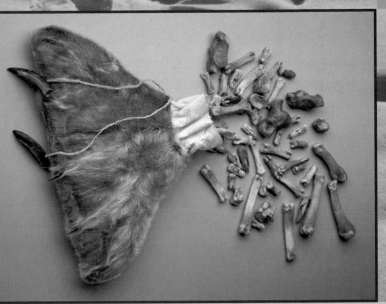

Bone Games

Inugait (shown above) are seal flipper bones used to play a traditional Inuit storytelling game. Each bone represented something different, such as part of an igloo, an adult or child, a dog sled, or a caribou. The bones were kept in a bag made from sealskin or the hollowed-out feet of a water bird (also pictured). In one variation of this game, adults would tell a story and then children would use a string with a loop to pull out of the bag the bones representing characters in the story.

An Inuit woman uses shapes made from string to illustrate a story.

String Games and Storytelling

Inuit legends and stories told about history and about the challenges of life in the Arctic, and offered lessons on how to be a good person. The stories might be accompanied by a string game called *ajaraat*, similar to "cat's cradle." The string was used to create shapes that represented characters in the stories.

Dolls

Making dolls is an ancient Inuit tradition. Fathers usually carved the dolls from driftwood. Using scraps of animal skin and fur, mothers helped their daughters make clothing for the dolls. In this way, young girls learned the skills of cutting and sewing skins and fur. When she was older, a girl would need these skills to make clothing for her family.

A hunter might attach his daughter's dolls to his kayak or sled as good luck charms to help make sure the hunt was successful. The dolls also encouraged the hunter by reminding him of his children, who were waiting for him to return with food for the family.

HUNTING

Traditional Inuit depended almost entirely on animals for food, so hunters needed effective hunting tools. They crafted a variety of tools for hunting different animals. By carefully observing each kind of animal, they discovered the best way to hunt it.

Today, Inuit hunters use rifles. But, like traditional Inuit, they still hunt for seals at breathing holes.

A hunter prepares to throw his harpoon.

This hunter has caught a beluga whale by using a harpoon with a sealskin float called an *avataq*.

Modern whale-hunting harpoons are often launched from a cannon on a ship.

Parts of a Harpoon

The harpoon was used for hunting sea mammals such as whales and seals. A traditional harpoon used for hunting on the sea had five parts:

1. The **long shaft** was the main part of the harpoon and was usually made of wood.
2. The **fore-shaft** was shorter than the long shaft, and was attached to the top of it. It was usually made of ivory or antler.
3. The **harpoon head** was often made from bone, and was attached to the end of the fore-shaft. The tip of the head had a sharp point or blade to pierce the animal.
4. A long length of **line**, made from sealskin, attached the harpoon head to the float.
5. The **float**, called an *avataq*, was made from the complete skin of a single seal, filled with air and plugged with a piece of ivory.

Hunting with a Harpoon

The hunter held on to the long shaft when preparing to throw the harpoon from his kayak. When the harpoon hit the animal, the harpoon head on the fore-shaft stuck into the animal's body. The long shaft then separated from the fore-shaft. The wooden long shaft would float so the hunter would not lose it. The float prevented a dead animal from sinking to the bottom of the sea.

When the sea is covered with ice, seals come to the surface to breathe at holes in the ice. These breathing holes are excellent places to hunt seals—something Inuit learned from watching polar bears catch seals. A group of hunters looked for an area where there were several breathing holes. Each hunter would wait, with a harpoon ready, at one of the holes. It was important to sit quietly without moving, sometimes for hours at a time, so as not to scare away any seals.

Fishing Spear and Fishing Weir

To catch fish, traditional Inuit developed a special kind of spear called a *kakivak*. A *kakivak* was made by attaching two pieces of caribou antler to the end of a long wooden pole. These pieces of antler were shaped into two prongs that grabbed onto the fish. A long spike between the prongs speared the fish. When used skillfully, the *kakivak* pulled a fish out of the water on the first try.

Inuit also used fishing methods found in other cultures. These included using a line with a hook at the end, and fishing nets, along with building weirs. Weirs are stone walls that direct fish to shallow water where they are easier to catch. In some places, Inuit used weirs that had been built long before by their ancestors.

An Inuit fishes through a hole in the ice. A *kakivak* can be seen lying on the snow.

Inuksuk

An *Inuksuk* (plural: *Inuksuit*) is a pile of stones that served as a guide for Inuit travelers. A traditional Inuit might build an *Inuksuk* to offer directions or to give information about good places to hunt caribou. A hunter might build a temporary *Inuksuk* to mark the place he has stored his caribou meat.

Inunnguat

Some *Inuksuit* were built in the shape of a person. These were called *Inunnguat* (plural; singular, *Inunnguaq*), which means "pretend Inuit." They were sometimes used to help hunt caribou.

Traditional hunters knew the paths that caribou took when they migrated from place to place. Where one of these paths was near a lake, the hunters would build several *Inunnguat* on either side of the path. When the caribou herd spotted the *Inunnguat*, they thought the stone figures were real hunters and ran away—toward the lake. The real Inuit would then jump out from hiding and wave their arms, which made the caribou stampede into the water. Hunters holding spears waited in kayaks on the lake. Caribou are much slower in water, so they were easier to hunt. The hunters on land used spears or bows and arrows.

FOOD

Traditional Inuit never knew when the next successful hunt would be, so it was important to safely store whatever food was on hand. Cold weather preserved food in the way that refrigerators and freezers do today, and Inuit developed methods for storing food during warmer months.

Raw Meat

For traditional Inuit, eating raw meat had two benefits: none of the meat's vitamins were destroyed during cooking, and Inuit did not have to use up valuable seal oil as a cooking fuel. Raw meat was easy to prepare and provided nutrients that helped keep people healthy enough to survive in the harsh Arctic land.

A young Arctic hunter enjoys a nutritious snack of raw seal eyeball.

Cooking

In the Arctic world of the Inuit, most cooking took place during the summer, when campfires could be made from driftwood and brush. But in the winter, heating fuel was scarce and Inuit had to rely on precious seal oil to burn in a *qulliq* (seal oil lamp; see page 17). A burning *qulliq* was the only source of heat and light inside the igloo during the cold, dark months of the year. Cooking with seal oil took a long time and was done only when there was plenty of the oil on hand. Meat and fish were boiled in a soapstone pot over the *qulliq*.

Ulu

The *ulu*, a traditional knife used by women, was one of the most useful tools ever invented in the Arctic. It was very effective for cutting frozen meat or fish. The curved shape of the blade and the position of the handle made it possible to use the strength of the muscles in the shoulder, arm, wrist, and hand to cut through frozen food.

The *ulu* was also used to cut seal and caribou skins to make clothes. By holding on to both sides of the blade, the user had better control when cutting. The skins were always cut on the inner, scraped side and not on the fur side to prevent any of the fur from accidentally being cut off.

Whale meat dries on wooden racks.

Food Preservation

In winter, the freezing of food kept it from going bad. But in summer, food had to be preserved in other ways to make it last longer. These ways included drying or storage in a sealskin bag.

Drying Food

Drying meat prevented it from going bad in warm weather. The quicker the meat dried, the safer it was to eat later. To help speed up the drying, all blood was drained from the meat. Next, the meat was cut into strips and hung on wooden racks to dry in the sunshine. After a day or two, the meat was ready to take down and store for later.

Inuit women cut up a beluga whale.

Once filled with food, sealskin bags were sealed and buried.

Storing Food in Sealskin

Meat and fish were sometimes preserved by storing them in an airtight sealskin bag with some seal blubber oil. The bag was buried and covered with rocks so animals could not dig it up. This method could preserve food from summer until it froze in winter.

Food stored high aboveground was safe from hungry animals, including the sled dogs.

Starvation

During times of starvation, old skins would sometimes become the last source of nutrients for traditional Inuit. In an emergency, skins were boiled to soften them so they could be eaten. At these desperate times, hungry husky dogs often gnawed at their sealskin harnesses.

MEDICINE AND HEALING

Traditional Inuit had no doctors or modern medicines to help them treat injuries and diseases. Instead, they developed their own remedies, using whatever was available in the Arctic.

Treating Frostbite

Inuit always needed to be careful in the intense cold of Arctic winters. Skin that is exposed to freezing temperatures for too long may develop a condition called frostbite, which can cause permanent damage.

To treat frostbite, Inuit held a warm hand over the affected area or soaked it in salt water or in cool urine. It was important to use a liquid that was not too hot, as this could cause more damage to the skin. Another remedy was to use dog droppings, wrapped in caribou skin and cloth, and then warmed by a fire before being applied to the frostbitten skin.

Frostbite has damaged this hunter's nose.

Inuit women harvest wild berries.

Wild cranberries grow in parts of the Arctic.

Sore Throat Remedies

There were several traditional remedies that Inuit used to treat a sore throat. They might eat raw or boiled cranberries, or chew some fat from a bearded seal and swallow the juice. Another treatment was to gargle with salt water, a remedy that doctors still recommend today. Sometimes the breast meat of a ptarmigan—a medium-sized bird with feathered feet—was placed on the neck before bedtime.

Treating Cuts and Scrapes

To treat cuts, scrapes, and other wounds, Inuit used materials they had at hand. Melted snow, freshwater algae, and even human urine could be used to safely clean open wounds. It was important to avoid getting salty sea water into a cut, as this could cause infection.

Once the wound had been cleaned, fat from a seal, caribou, or bird—such as an owl—was held against it to stop the bleeding. Then a thin slice of seal or caribou meat was laid on the cut for a few days to help it heal.

To help close a wound, Inuit traditionally used chewed gum from a pine tree or the insides of lice found in codfish. These sticky substances helped to keep the wound closed, much like stitches do.

Snow Goggles

Sunlight reflected off snow or ice can cause a temporary but painful blindness called "snow blindness." Today, skiers use tinted goggles to protect their eyes. But long before these were invented, traditional Inuit found a way to prevent snow blindness—with snow goggles made from wood, antler, or ivory. The goggles had a thin slit over each eye. These slits were large enough to see through, but they protected the eyes by preventing too much light from passing through.

Traditional Inuit snow goggles protected the eyes from snow blindness.

Mosquito Repellent

Swarms of mosquitoes were a big problem in summer. Even on the warmest days, hunters wore their parkas with the hoods up to keep from being bitten. Each hunter carried a small piece of caribou skin, like a handkerchief, to wave mosquitoes away.

Mosquitoes do not like smoke, so hunters would stay close to the campfire. They kept their dogs nearby too, as mosquitoes could take enough blood from a dog to kill it. At night, the dogs slept with the hunters inside tents that kept mosquitoes out.

Death Customs

Inuit in different areas of the Arctic had different customs related to death. Because much of the Arctic is rocky or permanently frozen, the dead were not buried. The body was left uncovered, or it might be covered with driftwood or a pile of rocks (as shown here).

Sometimes the body was placed inside a circle of small stones. Tools belonging to the dead person were placed with the body. If some of these tools could not be spared, miniature copies were used instead.

INUIT TODAY

Today, Inuit communities enjoy all the modern conveniences and the latest in technology. Some new technologies provide innovative ways of preserving and sharing Inuit traditions.

From the Past to the Present

Most of the amazing innovations described in this book were developed by traditional Inuit to help them survive and stay healthy in the harsh conditions of the Arctic. Hunting was an essential skill because animals provided traditional Inuit with the most basic necessities of life—not just food and clothing, but also hunting tools, materials for dog sleds and kayaks, summer shelters, and heating fuel, to name just a few. Survival depended on successful hunting.

For Inuit today, life is quite different. Instead of living in igloos and tents, we have modern heated homes with electricity. And we no longer depend on Arctic animals for survival; food, clothes, medicine, and all the conveniences of modern life can be purchased from stores. For transportation we use cars, snowmobiles, and motorboats rather than dog sleds and kayaks. Old and young alike enjoy many of the forms of entertainment that are probably in your home, such as TVs, MP3 players, CD and DVD players, and computer and video games.

These students use a computer to write in the traditional Inuktitut language.

In today's Inuit communities, people enjoy modern conveniences such as electrical power, heated buildings, and motorboats.

Modern Life and Inuit Culture

Traditional Inuit showed their unique ability to adapt to their surroundings in such useful innovations as the kayak, the double-bladed paddle, and the parka. These inventions were so successful that they are now used around the world. Today, Inuit show the same spirit of innovation in the ways in which we work to preserve our traditional culture while living a modern lifestyle.

Many Inuit children go to modern schools where they learn in the traditional language of Inuktitut. Some Inuit still include traditional foods such as caribou and fish in their diet, but hunters now use modern hunting technology in combination with traditional knowledge of the best ways and places to hunt. Inuit have developed websites in Inuktitut, and in other languages to share our Inuit culture—both traditional and modern—with communities around the world. And as the future brings even more changes, my people will continue to innovate and adapt, to move ahead with the times while preserving and strengthening the traditions of our past.

Snowmobiles are a useful form of transportation in the Arctic. Along with traditional Inuit sports, modern sports such as hockey are popular.

Some Inuit Communities Today

Further Reading

Corriveau, Danielle. *The Inuit of Canada*. Minneapolis: Lerner Publications, 2001.

Love, Ann, and Jane Drake. *The Kids Book of the Far North*. Toronto: Kids Can Press, 2000.

Reynolds, Jan. *Frozen Land: Vanishing Cultures*. New York: Harcourt, 1993.

Shemie, Bonnie. *Houses of snow, skin and bones*. Toronto: Tundra Books, 1989.

Tookoome, Simon, and Sheldon Oberman. *The Shaman's Nephew: A Life in the Far North*. Markham, ON: Fitzhenry and Whiteside, 1999.

Wallace, Mary. *The Inuksuk Book*. Toronto: Maple Tree Press, 1999.

Williams, Suzanne M. *The Inuit*. New York: Scholastic, 2003.

Yue, Charlotte and David. *The Igloo*. New York: Houghton Mifflin, 1988.

A Note on the Symbols Used in This Book

On each page of this book, you'll find symbols called syllabics that are part of the Inuktitut language. This is the traditional language of many Inuit, and it is still spoken today. Books and websites for Inuit often use this form of Inuktitut, while others use Inuktitut written using the letters of the English alphabet.

Inuktitut symbols are not the same as letters. In English, each letter stands for a sound, and letters are combined to make a syllable. In Inuktitut, each symbol stands for a whole syllable. The chart below shows the symbols used in Inuktitut and their matching spellings in the English alphabet.

ᐃ ᐄ	i ii	ᐅ ᐆ	u uu	ᐊ ᐋ	a aa	ᕼ	h
ᐱ ᐲ	pi pii	ᐳ ᐴ	pu puu	ᐸ ᐹ	pa paa	ᑉ	p
ᑎ ᑏ	ti tii	ᑐ ᑑ	tu tuu	ᑕ ᑖ	ta taa	ᑦ	t
ᑭ ᑮ	ki kii	ᑯ ᑰ	ku kuu	ᑲ ᑳ	ka kaa	ᒃ	k
ᒋ ᒌ	gi gii	ᒍ ᒎ	gu guu	ᒐ ᒑ	ga gaa	ᒡ	g
ᒥ ᒦ	mi mii	ᒧ ᒨ	mu muu	ᒪ ᒫ	ma maa	ᒻ	m
ᓂ ᓃ	ni nii	ᓄ ᓅ	nu nuu	ᓇ ᓈ	na naa	ᓐ	n
ᓯ ᓰ	si sii	ᓱ ᓲ	su suu	ᓴ ᓵ	sa saa	ᔅ	s
ᓕ ᓖ	li lii	ᓗ ᓘ	lu luu	ᓚ ᓛ	la laa	ᓪ	l
ᔨ ᔩ	ji jii	ᔪ ᔫ	ju juu	ᔭ ᔮ	ja jaa	ᔾ	j
ᕕ ᕖ	vi vii	ᕗ ᕘ	vu vuu	ᕙ ᕚ	va vaa	ᕝ	v
ᕆ ᕇ	ri rii	ᕈ ᕉ	ru ruu	ᕋ ᕌ	ra raa	ᕐ	r
ᕿ ᖀ	qi qii	ᖁ ᖂ	qu quu	ᖃ ᖄ	qa qaa	ᖅ	q
ᖏ ᖐ	ngi ngii	ᖑ ᖒ	ngu nguu	ᖓ ᖔ	nga ngaa	ᖕ	ng
ᙱ ᙲ	nngi nngii	ᙳ ᙴ	nngu nnguu	ᙵ ᙶ	nnga nngaa	ᖖ	nng
ᖠ ᖡ	&i &ii	ᖢ ᖣ	&u &uu	ᖤ ᖥ	&a &aa	ᖦ	&

Credits

Cover top, Snow Goggles ©Canadian Museum of Civilization, IX-C-2846, photo Ross Taylor, image number S89-1832; **17 right,** Sleeping Bag ©Canadian Museum of Civilization, IV-C-3192, image number D2004-06629; **19 right,** Boots ©Canadian Museum of Civilization, IV-C-2916 a, b, image number S96-05817; **21 top,** Bone Game ©Canadian Museum of Civilization, IV-C-4625, image number S95-21340; **21 bottom,** Dolls ©Canadian Museum of Civilization, IV-B-756 a–c, image number S95-25043

Cover middle, ©iStockphoto Inc./Miha Urbanija; **3, back cover third,** ©iStockphoto Inc./ChoiceGraphX; **5 right top, 14 bottom background, 20 top, 27 background, back cover second background,** ©iStockphoto Inc./Gregor Kervina; **5 left middle, back cover top,** ©iStockphoto Inc./Shaun Lowe; **6 top, 7 top,** ©iStockphoto Inc./Matthias Frhr. v. Sohlern; **6 top left,** ©iStockphoto Inc./John Pitcher; **7 top right,** ©iStockphoto Inc./Roman Krochuk; **11 top,** ©iStockphoto Inc./Vera Bogaerts, **12 right,** ©iStockphoto Inc./Eric Coia; **12 left,** ©iStockphoto Inc./Roman Krochuk; **13 top background, 15 background, 18 bottom background, back cover third background,** ©iStockphoto Inc./Dmitry Goygel-Sokol; **16 middle left background, back cover fourth background,** ©iStockphoto Inc./Simon Edwin; **16 bottom, 25 main background,** ©iStockphoto Inc./Annette Diekmann; **17 bottom,** ©iStockphoto Inc./Elisa Locci; **19 right background, 22 bottom background,** ©iStockphoto Inc./Carmen Martínez Banús; **19 bottom left,** ©iStockphoto Inc./Josef Volavka; **22 bottom,** ©iStockphoto Inc./Chris Overgaard; **23 right, 29 background,** ©iStockphoto Inc./Zastavkin; **26 left bottom,** ©iStockphoto Inc./Chris Hill; **27 left top,** ©iStockphoto Inc./Maartje van Caspel

Cover bottom, ©B & C Alexander/Arcticphoto.com; **27 right,** ©B & C Alexander/Arcticphoto.com; **28 top,** ©B & C Alexander/Arcticphoto.com

4, Alaska Yukon Pacific Exposition/Frank H. Nowell, LC-USZ62-101171; **7 bottom right,** LOT 11453-1, no. 53; **8 bottom,** Edward S. Curtis Collection, LC-USZ62-16892; **12–13 main background,** LC-USZ62-133487; **13 middle,** Edward S. Curtis Collection, LC-USZ62-107284; **14 top,** Edward S. Curtis Collection, LC-USZ62-107287; **14 middle,** Edward S. Curtis Collection, LC-USZ62-107323; **15 middle right,** Edward S. Curtis Collection, LC-USZ62-89845; **15 middle left,** LC-USZ62-103527; **16 middle right, back cover fourth,** Frank E. Kleinschmidt, LC-USZ62-135985; **17 top,** Edward S. Curtis, photographer, LC-USZ62-101338; **18 top,** Edward S. Curtis Collection, LC-USZ62-89847; **18 middle left,** LOT 11453-6, no. 6; **18 bottom,** LC-USZ62-68745; **19 top left,** Edward S. Curtis Collection, LC-USZ62-130414; **20 middle,** LC-USZ62-133489; **22 middle,** Edward S. Curtis Collection, LC-USZ62-13912; **23 left background,** LC-USZ62-112765; **24 top right,** LOT 11453-3, no. 7; **25 top right,** Edward S. Curtis Collection, LC-USZ62-101258; **25 middle right,** Edward S. Curtis Collection, LOT 12330; **25 bottom right,** LOT 11453-5, no. 6; **25 left,** Edward S. Curtis Collection, LC-USZ62-116541; **26 left top,** Edward S. Curtis Collection, LC-USZ62-67382. All courtesy Library of Congress, Prints & Photographs Division.

5 right bottom, 17 top background, 28 bottom background, back cover top background, Arctic National Wildlife Refuge; **8 top,** Yukon Delta National Wildlife Refuge; **8 middle,** Keith Morehouse, Division of Public Affairs; **10,** Mike Spindler; **11 bottom,** Scott Schliebe, Division of Public Affairs; **12 left background, 21 top background,** Greg Weiler, Division of Public Affairs; **21 bottom background,** Yukon Delta National Wildlife Refuge; **18 top background,** Arctic National Wildlife Refuge; **24 bottom background,** Luther Goldman, Division of Public Affairs; **25 far right background, 27 left bottom,** Anne Morkill, Alaska Maritime National Wildlife Refuge. All courtesy U.S. Fish and Wildlife Service.

5 left top, Richard S. Finnie/Library and Archives Canada/e002342733; **5 left bottom,** ©Library and Archives Canada. Reproduced with the permission of Library and Archives Canada. Richard Harrington/Richard Harrington fonds/Accession 1976-086 NPC/PA-114686; **6 bottom left,** ©Library and Archives Canada. Reproduced with the permission of Library and Archives Canada. Richard Harrington/Richard Harrington fonds/Accession 1976-086 NPC/PA-114706; **13 top, back cover second,** ©Library and Archives Canada. Reproduced with the permission of Library and Archives Canada. Richard Harrington/Richard Harrington fonds/Accession 1976-086 NPC/PA-146785; **13 bottom,** ©Library and Archives Canada. Reproduced with the permission of Library and Archives Canada. Charles Gimpel/Charles Gimpel fonds/e004922696; **14 bottom,** Library and Archives Canada/PA-042120; **15 top,** R.S. Finnie/Library and Archives Canada/PA-100751; **16 top,** ©Library and Archives Canada. Reproduced with the permission of Library and Archives Canada. Richard Harrington/Richard Harrington fonds/Accession 1976-086 NPC/PA-114707; **16 middle left,** ©Library and Archives Canada. Reproduced with the permission of Library and Archives Canada. Richard Harrington/Richard Harrington fonds/Accession 1976-086 NPC/PA-114656; **17 left,** ©Health Canada. Reproduced with the permission of the Minister of Public Works and Government Services Canada (2006). Library and Archives Canada/Department of National Health and Welfare fonds/R227-213-1E/Accession 1997-309 NPC/e002394409; **18 middle right,** National Film Board of Canada. Photothèque/Library and Archives Canada/PA-146508; **19 middle left,** National Film Board of Canada. Photothèque/Library and Archives Canada/PA-145968; **21 middle,** ©Library and Archives Canada. Reproduced with the permission of Library and Archives Canada. Richard Harrington/Richard Harrington fonds/Accession 1976-086 NPC/PA-114667; **22 middle background,** George Simpson McTavish/Library and Archives Canada/C-022942; **23 middle,** ©Library and Archives Canada. Reproduced with the permission of Library and Archives Canada. Richard Harrington/Richard Harrington fonds/Accession 1976-086 NPC/PA-112088; **23 left,** ©Library and Archives Canada. Reproduced with the permission of Library and Archives Canada. Richard Harrington/Richard Harrington fonds/Accession 1976-086 NPC/PA-114695; **26 right,** ©Library and Archives Canada. Reproduced with the permission of Library and Archives Canada. Richard Harrington/Richard Harrington fonds/Accession 1976-086 NPC/PA-114728; **27 left middle,** ©Library and Archives Canada. Reproduced with the permission of Library and Archives Canada. Richard Harrington/Richard Harrington fonds/Accession 1976-086 NPC/PA-129886

15 bottom, ©Wally McNamee/CORBIS; **20 bottom,** ©Lowell Georgia/CORBIS; **22 top,** ©Staffan Widstrand/CORBIS; **24 top left,** ©Staffan Widstrand/CORBIS; **24 bottom,** ©Staffan Widstrand/CORBIS; **28 bottom,** ©Alison Wright/CORBIS; **29,** ©Wolfgang Kaehler/CORBIS

23 bottom, Art by Tim Yearington

Selected Bibliography

The following reference sources were particularly helpful.

For the timeline:

Aboriginal Innovations in Arts, Science and Technology: A Public Education Initiative of Lakehead University, The Lakehead University Native Student Association and the Department of Indian and Northern Affairs Canada. Thunder Bay: Lakehead University, 2002. http://www.schoolnet.ca/aboriginal/handbook/about-e.html

Canadian Museum of Civilization website: www.civilization.ca

McGhee, Robert. *Canadian Arctic Prehistory*. Toronto: Van Nostrand Reinhold, 1978.

Morrison, David, and Georges-Hébert Germain. *Inuit: Glimpses of an Arctic Past*. Illustrations by Frédéric Back. Canadian Museum of Civilization, 1995.

For the maps:

Canada: Inuit Identity Population by 2001 Census Subdivision. Geography Division, Statistics Canada, 2002.

Map of North America by Tourizm Maps © 2003 http://www.world-maps.co.uk/continent-map-of-north-america.htm

Map of Nunavut Communities. Natural Resources Canada: http://atlas.nrcan.gc.ca/site/english/index.html

McGhee, Robert. *Canadian Arctic Prehistory*. Toronto: Van Nostrand Reinhold, 1978.

Statistics Canada. 2007. *2006 Community Profiles*. 2006 Census. Statistics Canada Catalogue no. 92-591-XWE. Ottawa. Released March 13, 2007. http://www12.statcan.ca/english/census06/data/profiles/community/Index.cfm?Lang=E (accessed June 14, 2007).

The Eskimo-Aleut Family Map. The Tower of Babel: An International Etymological Database Project: http://starling.rinet.ru/maps/maps7.php?lan=en

Where the Inuit Live—The Arctic. National Atlas Information Service, Canada Centre for Mapping, Natural Resources Canada.

For the Inuktitut language chart:

Nortext, *Nunacom Character Combination Chart*: http://www.nunavut.com/nunacom/charchart.html

Timwi, *The syllabary used to write Inuktitut (titirausiq nutaaq)*: http://commons.wikimedia.org/wiki/Image:Inuktitut.png

As reference material can be difficult to find on the subject, some sources consulted for the Medicine and Healing chapter:

Avataq Cultural Institute. *Traditional Medicine Project, Interim Report*. Montreal: September 28, 1983.

Ootoova, Ilisapi, et al. *Perspectives on Traditional Health*. Interviewing Inuit Elders 5. Edited by Michèle Therrien and Frédéric Laugrand. Iqaluit: Nunavut Arctic College, 2001.

Index